The SEO Guid Mastering the Art of Search Engine Optimisation

By Adam J Broadhead

Introduction

Welcome to "The SEO Guide 2023: Mastering the Art of Search Engine Optimisation" - your comprehensive guide to understanding, implementing, and staying ahead in the ever-changing world of SEO. This book is designed to equip you with the knowledge and skills you need to succeed in the digital landscape and drive targeted traffic to your website. Whether you're a business owner, marketer, or aspiring SEO professional, this guide will provide you with the latest insights, strategies, and best practices to help you rank higher in search engine results and boost your online presence.

SEO, or search engine optimisation, is the process of improving your website's visibility in search engine results pages (SERPs). The primary goal of SEO is to increase organic (non-paid) traffic to your website, resulting in more leads, conversions, and ultimately, revenue. As the internet continues to grow and evolve, it's crucial to adapt your SEO strategies to keep up with the latest trends and best practices.

This book is divided into 15 chapters, each covering a specific aspect of SEO. In the first chapter, we'll take a brief look at the history of SEO and how it has evolved over time. From there, we'll delve into the inner workings of search engines, including their algorithms and ranking factors. In chapters three to nine, we'll cover the essential components of SEO, such as keyword research, on-page and off-page optimisation, technical SEO, content marketing, local SEO, and mobile SEO. We'll also discuss the emerging importance of voice search and how you can prepare your website for this growing trend.

Next, we'll explore SEO analytics and the tools and resources available to help you track your progress, measure success, and maximise your efficiency. In chapter 13, we'll discuss the future of SEO, with a focus on trends and predictions for the coming years. Chapter 14 will address penalties and recovery, ensuring you stay on the right side of search engines and maintain a healthy online presence.

Finally, in chapter 15, we'll bring it all together, helping you develop a comprehensive and effective SEO strategy to drive your online success.

Throughout this book, you'll find a confident and informative writing style, providing you with actionable insights, tips, and advice to help you stay ahead of the competition. So, without further ado, let's dive in and begin our journey to mastering the art of search engine optimisation.

Table of Contents

Chapter 1: The Evolution of SEO: A Brief History 12

1.1 The Early Days of Search Engines 12

    1.2 The Emergence of Google 12

    1.3 The Rise of SEO 13

    1.4 The Evolution of Search Algorithms 13

1.5 The Modern SEO Landscape 14

Chapter 2: Understanding Search Engines: Algorithms and Ranking Factors 16

    2.1 How Search Engines Work 16

    2.2 Search Engine Algorithms 17

    2.3 On-Site vs. Off-Site Ranking Factors 17

    2.4 Understanding and Adapting to Algorithm Updates 18

Chapter 3: Keyword Research: Finding the Right Words for Your Audience 20

    3.1 The Importance of Keyword Research 20

    3.2 Understanding Search Intent 21

    3.4 Incorporating Keywords into Your Content 22

    3.5 Long-Tail Keywords: The Key to Targeted Traffic 24

Chapter 4: On-Page SEO: Optimising Your Website for Search Engines and Users 25

    4.1 Keyword Optimisation: Getting the Most Out of Your Content 25

    4.2 Content Quality: Creating Valuable, Engaging Content for Your Audience 26

4.3 Technical Performance: Ensuring Your Website Loads Quickly and Functions Properly 27

4.5 Schema Markup: Helping Search Engines Understand Your Content 28

Chapter 5: Off-Page SEO: Building Authority and Trust with Search Engines...31

5.1 Backlinks: The Foundation of Off-Page SEO 31

5.2 Social Signals: The Impact of Social Media on SEO.......32

5.3 Online Reputation Management: Protecting and Enhancing Your Brand Image 33

Chapter 6: Local SEO: Optimising Your Website for Local Search Results 35

6.1 Google My Business: The Foundation of Local SEO......35

6.2 Local Keyword Research: Identifying Target Keywords for Your Geographic Area 36

6.3 On-Page Local SEO: Optimising Your Website for Local Search Results 37

Chapter 7: Technical SEO: Ensuring Your Website Performs Well for Users and Search Engines..39

7.1 Site Speed: The Importance of a Fast-Loading Website 39

7.2 Mobile-Friendliness: Catering to the Growing Mobile Audience..40

7.3 Structured Data: Helping Search Engines Understand Your Content 41

Chapter 8: Content Marketing: Attracting and Engaging Your Target Audience with Valuable Content...................................43

8.1 Content Planning: Developing a Strategic Approach to Your Content 43

8.2 Content Creation: Crafting High-Quality, Valuable Content 44

8.3 Content Promotion: Maximising the Reach and Visibility of Your Content 45

Chapter 9: Analytics and Performance Tracking: Measuring and Optimising Your SEO Efforts 46

9.1 Google Analytics: Monitoring Your Website's Traffic and User Behaviour 46

9.2 Google Search Console: Gaining Insights into Your Website's Search Performance 47

9.3 Key Performance Indicators (KPIs): Tracking the Success of Your SEO Efforts 48

Chapter 10: Ongoing SEO Maintenance: Keeping Your Website Optimised and Competitive 50

10.1 Staying Updated with Algorithm Changes: Adapting to the Evolving Search Landscape 50

10.2 Ongoing Link Building: Continuously Building and Maintaining Your Website's Backlink Profile 51

10.3 Updating and Refreshing Your Content: Keeping Your Website Relevant and Engaging 52

Chapter 11: Advanced SEO Techniques: Taking Your Website's Performance to the Next Level 54

11.1 Schema Markup: Enhancing Your Search Results with Structured Data 54

11.2 Local SEO: Optimising Your Website for Local Search and Visibility 55

11.3 Mobile-First Indexing: Ensuring Your Website is Optimised for Mobile Devices 56

Chapter 12: Social Media and SEO: Leveraging Social Platforms to Support Your SEO Efforts 57

12.1 Social Signals: Understanding the Impact of Social Media on SEO 57

12.2 Content Promotion: Using Social Media to Drive Traffic and Engagement 58

12.3 Social Listening: Monitoring Social Media for SEO Insights and Opportunities 59

Chapter 13: Continuous Learning and Professional Development in SEO 60

13.1 The Importance of Continuous Learning in SEO 60

13.2 Recommended SEO Resources and Publications 61

13.3 Networking and Community Involvement in the SEO Industry 61

Chapter 14: SEO Guide Recap: Key Takeaways and Actionable Steps 63

Chapter 15: Measuring SEO Success and Adjusting Your Strategy 66

15.1 Key Performance Indicators (KPIs) to Track 66

15.2 Tools for Measuring Your Website's Performance 67

15.3 Adjusting Your SEO Strategy Based on Data-Driven Insights 67

Chapter 1: The Evolution of SEO: A Brief History

In this chapter, we'll explore the origins of search engine optimisation and its evolution over the years, providing you with a solid foundation to understand how SEO has become the crucial digital marketing strategy it is today.

1.1 The Early Days of Search Engines

The history of SEO can be traced back to the 1990s when the first search engines were introduced. In the beginning, search engines like Archie, Veronica, and Jughead relied on simple algorithms to index and retrieve web pages. These early search engines used basic keyword matching techniques to rank pages in search results, making it relatively easy for webmasters to manipulate rankings.

1.2 The Emergence of Google

The game changed in 1998 when Google was introduced, offering a new approach to search engine algorithms. Google's PageRank algorithm revolutionised the search landscape by considering not only the content of a page but also the number and quality of links pointing to it. This innovation made it more difficult for webmasters to manipulate rankings and laid the groundwork for the complex, ever-evolving world of SEO we know today.

1.3 The Rise of SEO

As search engines became more advanced and their algorithms more sophisticated, the need for SEO grew. Webmasters and marketers quickly recognised the value of ranking highly in search results and began to develop strategies to improve their website's visibility. Initially, these strategies were fairly simple, focusing on keyword optimisation and building backlinks.

1.4 The Evolution of Search Algorithms

Over the years, search engines have continued to update and refine their algorithms to provide users with the most relevant and valuable results. These updates have forced webmasters and marketers to adapt their SEO strategies accordingly. Some notable algorithm updates include:

- Google Panda (2011): Targeted low-quality content, rewarding sites with high-quality, original content.
- Google Penguin (2012): Focused on penalising websites with unnatural link profiles, encouraging ethical link-building practices.

- Google Hummingbird (2013): Improved the understanding of user intent and context, rewarding sites with relevant and in-depth content.
- Google Mobilegeddon (2015): Prioritised mobile-friendly websites in mobile search results, signalling the growing importance of mobile optimisation.
- Google RankBrain (2015): Introduced machine learning to better understand user queries and refine search results.

1.5 The Modern SEO Landscape

Today, the world of SEO is more complex than ever, with hundreds of ranking factors and countless strategies to consider. Webmasters and marketers must focus not only on keyword optimisation and link-building but also on user experience, content quality, technical performance, and more. As search engines become more sophisticated and user demands evolve, the importance of staying ahead of the curve in SEO continues to grow.

In the next chapter, we'll delve deeper into the inner workings of search engines, exploring the algorithms and ranking factors that drive search results and shape the modern SEO landscape.

Chapter 2: Understanding Search Engines: Algorithms and Ranking Factors

In this chapter, we'll explore how search engines work, focusing on the algorithms and ranking factors that determine the visibility of your website in search results.

2.1 How Search Engines Work

Search engines like Google, Bing, and Yahoo use automated programs called crawlers or spiders to discover and index web pages. These crawlers follow links from one page to another, collecting information about each page they visit. This information is then stored in a massive database called an index, which is used to serve search results to users.

When a user types a query into a search engine, the search engine's algorithm sifts through its index to find the most relevant and valuable pages for that query. These pages are then ranked in search results based on a variety of factors, such as their relevance

to the query, the quality of their content, and the number and quality of links pointing to them. The higher a page ranks in search results, the more likely it is to be clicked on by users, driving organic traffic to the website.

2.2 Search Engine Algorithms

Search engine algorithms are complex mathematical formulas that determine how pages are ranked in search results. These algorithms consider hundreds of different factors, known as ranking factors, which are weighted differently depending on their importance. Some of the most significant ranking factors include:

- **Relevance:** How closely a page's content matches the user's query.
- **Quality:** The overall quality, depth, and value of a page's content.
- **Authority:** The number and quality of links pointing to a page, indicating its credibility and trustworthiness.
- **User experience:** How easy and enjoyable it is for users to interact with a page, including factors like page load time, mobile-friendliness, and readability.

Search engine algorithms are constantly updated and refined to provide users with the best possible search experience. These updates often require webmasters and marketers to adjust their SEO strategies to maintain or improve their website's visibility in search results.

2.3 On-Site vs. Off-Site Ranking Factors

Ranking factors can be broadly categorised into two groups: on-site factors and off-site factors.

On-site factors are those related to the content, structure, and design of a website. These factors include keyword optimisation, meta tags, header tags, URL structure, internal linking, and more. On-site factors are crucial for ensuring that search engines understand the content of your website and can accurately match it to relevant user queries.

Off-site factors, on the other hand, are those related to the external signals that search engines use to assess a website's credibility and trustworthiness. These factors include backlinks, social signals, and online reviews. Off-site factors are important for building authority and trust with search engines, helping to improve your website's overall visibility and ranking potential.

2.4 Understanding and Adapting to Algorithm Updates

As mentioned earlier, search engine algorithms are constantly updated to provide users with the best possible search experience. These updates can have a significant impact on your website's visibility and performance in search results, making it essential to stay informed and adapt your SEO strategy accordingly.

To stay ahead of algorithm updates, it's important to:

- **Stay informed:** Follow industry news and search engine announcements to learn about algorithm updates and their potential impact on your website.
- **Monitor your website's performance:** Regularly track your website's visibility, traffic, and rankings to identify any changes or fluctuations that may indicate an algorithm update.
- **Adapt your strategy:** If your website's performance is negatively impacted by an algorithm update, review your SEO strategy and make any necessary adjustments to get back on track.

In the next chapter, we'll dive into one of the most critical aspects of SEO: keyword research. We'll explore how to find the right keywords for your audience and incorporate them into your website to improve your visibility and ranking potential in search results.

Chapter 3: Keyword Research: Finding the Right Words for Your Audience

In this chapter, we'll explore the process of keyword research, an essential component of any successful SEO strategy. We'll discuss the importance of choosing the right keywords for your audience and provide practical tips and tools to help you identify the most valuable and relevant keywords for your website.

3.1 The Importance of Keyword Research

Keywords are the foundation of SEO, as they represent the terms and phrases that users type into search engines when looking for information, products, or services. By optimising your website for the right keywords, you can ensure that your content reaches the right audience, driving targeted traffic to your site and increasing the likelihood of conversions.

Keyword research involves identifying the terms and phrases that are most relevant to your business and target audience, allowing you to create content that matches their search intent. By targeting the right keywords, you can improve your website's visibility, rankings, and overall performance in search results.

3.2 Understanding Search Intent

Search intent, or user intent, refers to the goal a user has in mind when typing a query into a search engine. Understanding search intent is crucial for selecting the most effective keywords for your website, as it helps ensure that your content aligns with the needs and expectations of your target audience.

There are four primary types of search intent:

- **Informational:** The user is looking for information on a specific topic or subject.
- **Navigational:** The user is trying to find a specific website or page.
- **Transactional:** The user is ready to make a purchase or complete a specific action.
- **Commercial investigation:** The user is researching products or services before making a decision.

When conducting keyword research, it's essential to consider the search intent behind each keyword and create content that addresses the specific needs and goals of your audience.

3.3 Keyword Research Tools and Techniques

There are several tools and techniques available to help you conduct effective keyword research. Some of the most popular keyword research tools include:

- **Google Keyword Planner:** A free tool provided by Google that allows you to find keyword ideas and search volume data based on your target audience, location, and industry.
- **SEMrush:** A comprehensive SEO tool that offers keyword research, competitor analysis, and other features to help you optimise your website.
- **Ahrefs:** Another powerful SEO tool that provides keyword research, backlink analysis, and more to help you improve your website's performance in search results.
- **Moz Keyword Explorer:** A user-friendly keyword research tool that offers keyword suggestions, search volume data, and keyword difficulty scores.

When using these tools, it's essential to consider factors such as search volume, keyword difficulty, and relevance to your target audience. Look for keywords with a high search volume and low to medium competition, as these will offer the best opportunity for your website to rank well in search results.

3.4 Incorporating Keywords into Your Content

Once you have identified the most valuable and relevant keywords for your website, it's crucial to incorporate them into your content in a natural and strategic manner. This includes placing keywords in your:

- **Title tags:** These are the HTML elements that define the title of your web pages and appear as clickable headlines in search results.
- **Meta descriptions:** These are the brief summaries of your web pages that appear below the title tags in search results.
- **Header tags:** These are the HTML elements used to structure your content and indicate the hierarchy of your headings and subheadings.
- **URL structure:** Your web page URLs should be descriptive, user-friendly, and include your target keywords.
- **Image file names and alt tags:** Include keywords in your image file names and alt tags to help search engines understand the content of your images.
- **Body content:** Naturally incorporate your target keywords throughout your content, ensuring that they flow seamlessly and provide value to your readers.

Remember, while it's essential to include keywords in your content, avoid keyword stuffing, which can lead to a negative user experience and potential penalties from search engines. Focus on creating high-quality, engaging content that addresses the needs and search intent of your target audience.

3.5 Long-Tail Keywords: The Key to Targeted Traffic

In addition to targeting popular, high-volume keywords, it's essential to focus on long-tail keywords, which are longer, more specific phrases that represent a smaller but more targeted portion of search traffic. Long-tail keywords often have lower search volumes and less competition, making it easier for your website to rank well in search results.

By targeting long-tail keywords, you can attract a more targeted audience with a higher likelihood of converting, as they're often searching for specific information, products, or services related to your business. To find long-tail keyword opportunities, use keyword research tools to identify more specific, niche phrases related to your primary keywords and create content that addresses the unique needs and search intent of these users.

In the next chapter, we'll explore on-page SEO, diving into the best practices and techniques for optimising your website's content, structure, and design to improve your visibility and performance in search results.

Chapter 4: On-Page SEO: Optimising Your Website for Search Engines and Users

In this chapter, we'll discuss on-page SEO, focusing on the best practices and techniques for optimising your website's content, structure, and design to improve your visibility and performance in search results. We'll cover everything from keyword optimisation to technical performance, ensuring you have the knowledge and tools to create an SEO-friendly website that ranks well in search results and provides a positive user experience.

4.1 Keyword Optimisation: Getting the Most Out of Your Content

As discussed in Chapter 3, keyword research is a crucial aspect of SEO, helping you identify the most valuable and relevant terms and phrases for your target audience. Once you have identified your target keywords, it's essential to incorporate them into your content in a natural and strategic manner, ensuring they flow seamlessly and provide value to your readers.

In addition to including keywords in your title tags, meta descriptions, header tags, URL structure, image file names, and alt tags, make sure to:

- Use your primary keyword early in your content, preferably within the first 100-150 words.
- Use variations and synonyms of your primary keyword to provide context and improve the overall relevance of your content.
- Keep keyword density in check, ensuring you don't overuse your target keywords and risk keyword stuffing.

4.2 Content Quality: Creating Valuable, Engaging Content for Your Audience

While keyword optimisation is crucial, it's just as important to create high-quality, engaging content that addresses the needs and search intent of your target audience. To ensure your content is valuable and engaging, focus on:

- Providing in-depth, well-researched information that answers users' questions and provides actionable insights.
- Using a clear, concise writing style that's easy to read and understand.
- Breaking up large blocks of text with headings, subheadings, images, and bullet points to improve readability.
- Updating your content regularly to ensure it remains accurate, relevant, and up-to-date.

4.3 Technical Performance: Ensuring Your Website Loads Quickly and Functions Properly

Technical performance is a critical aspect of on-page SEO, as it directly impacts your website's visibility in search results and the overall user experience. To optimise your website's technical performance, focus on:

- Reducing page load times by compressing images, minifying CSS and JavaScript files, and using caching and content delivery networks (CDNs).
- Ensuring your website is mobile-friendly and responsive, adapting to different devices and screen sizes to provide a seamless user experience.
- Implementing proper URL structures that are descriptive, user-friendly, and include your target keywords.
- Using clean, well-structured HTML and CSS to ensure your website is easily accessible and navigable for both users and search engines.
- Fixing broken links and addressing crawl errors to ensure search engines can efficiently index and rank your website.

4.4 Internal Linking: Connecting Your Content for Improved Navigation and SEO

Internal linking refers to the practice of linking your web pages to each other, helping users and search engines navigate your website and discover new content. Effective internal linking is crucial for on-page SEO, as it helps:

- Spread link equity (also known as link juice) across your website, improving the overall authority and ranking potential of your pages.
- Establish a clear, logical hierarchy for your content, making it easier for search engines to understand the structure and importance of your pages.
- Enhance the user experience by providing relevant, related content that users can explore to find additional information.

To implement an effective internal linking strategy, focus on:

- Creating a clear, logical site structure with a well-organised hierarchy of pages and categories.
- Using descriptive, keyword-rich anchor text for your internal links to provide context and improve relevance.
- Linking to your most important pages from your homepage and other high-authority pages to improve their visibility and ranking potential.
- Regularly reviewing and updating your internal links to ensure they remain accurate, relevant, and functional.

4.5 Schema Markup: Helping Search Engines Understand Your Content

Schema markup is a form of structured data that helps search engines better understand the content of your web pages, allowing them to provide richer, more informative search results for users. Implementing schema markup on your website can improve your visibility and click-through rates in search results, as well as enhance the overall user experience.

Some common types of schema markup include:

- **Organization**: Provides information about your business, such as your name, logo, and contact details.
- **Breadcrumbs**: Displays a breadcrumb trail in search results, helping users understand the structure and hierarchy of your website.
- **Article**: Highlights the main content of your web pages, including the headline, author, and publication date.
- **Product**: Provides detailed information about your products, including their name, price, and availability.

To implement schema markup on your website, use Google's Structured Data Markup Helper or a schema markup generator tool to create the appropriate code for your content, and add it to your website's HTML.

In the next chapter, we'll explore off-page SEO, focusing on the techniques and strategies for building authority and trust with search engines, improving your website's overall visibility and ranking potential in search results.

Chapter 5: Off-Page SEO: Building Authority and Trust with Search Engines

In this chapter, we'll discuss off-page SEO, focusing on the techniques and strategies for building authority and trust with search engines, ultimately improving your website's overall visibility and ranking potential in search results. We'll cover topics such as backlinks, social signals, and online reputation management, ensuring you have the knowledge and tools to create a successful off-page SEO strategy for your website.

5.1 Backlinks: The Foundation of Off-Page SEO

Backlinks, also known as inbound or incoming links, are links from other websites pointing to your website. They are a critical aspect of off-page SEO, as they serve as a vote of confidence or endorsement from other websites, helping search engines determine the credibility, trustworthiness, and authority of your website.

The quality, quantity, and relevance of your backlinks can significantly impact your website's visibility and performance in search results. To build a strong backlink profile, focus on:

- Creating high-quality, valuable content that other websites will want to link to.

- Building relationships with industry influencers, bloggers, and other relevant websites to encourage natural link building.
- Conducting outreach campaigns to promote your content and request links from relevant websites.
- Avoiding black-hat SEO techniques, such as link buying or participating in link schemes, which can lead to penalties from search engines.

5.2 Social Signals: The Impact of Social Media on SEO

Social signals, such as likes, shares, and comments, can also influence your website's off-page SEO, as they indicate the popularity and engagement of your content. While the direct impact of social signals on search engine rankings is a topic of ongoing debate, there's no denying that a strong social media presence can improve your website's overall visibility and reputation online.

To leverage the power of social media for off-page SEO, focus on:

- Sharing your content on relevant social media platforms, such as Facebook, Twitter, LinkedIn, and Pinterest, to increase its reach and visibility.
- Engaging with your audience on social media, responding to comments, and encouraging discussion to foster a sense of community and loyalty around your brand.

- Collaborating with influencers and industry experts to expand your reach and generate additional social signals for your content.

5.3 Online Reputation Management: Protecting and Enhancing Your Brand Image

Your online reputation can have a significant impact on your website's off-page SEO, as search engines use various signals to determine the trustworthiness and credibility of your website. To maintain a positive online reputation and protect your website's SEO potential, focus on:

- Monitoring your brand mentions and customer reviews on various platforms, such as social media, review websites, and industry forums.
- Addressing negative feedback and resolving customer complaints in a timely and professional manner.
- Encouraging satisfied customers to leave positive reviews and testimonials, which can help to counteract any negative feedback and improve your overall reputation.
- Implementing a proactive PR strategy to generate positive news and coverage for your brand, helping to build trust and authority with both search engines and users.

In the next chapter, we'll dive into the world of local SEO, discussing the techniques and strategies for optimising your website for local search results and attracting customers from your target geographic area.

Chapter 6: Local SEO: Optimising Your Website for Local Search Results

In this chapter, we'll discuss local SEO, focusing on the techniques and strategies for optimising your website for local search results and attracting customers from your target geographic area. We'll cover topics such as Google My Business, local keyword research, and on-page local SEO tactics, ensuring you have the knowledge and tools to create a successful local SEO strategy for your website.

6.1 Google My Business: The Foundation of Local SEO

Google My Business (GMB) is a free tool that allows businesses to manage their online presence on Google, including Search and Maps. Creating and optimising a GMB listing is a crucial aspect of local SEO, as it can improve your visibility in local search results and help potential customers find and engage with your business.

To set up and optimise your GMB listing, focus on:

- Claiming your business listing on Google My Business, providing accurate and up-to-date information about your business, such as your name, address, phone number, and website.

- Choosing the most relevant business category and subcategories to help Google understand the nature of your business and display your listing for relevant local searches.
- Adding high-quality photos and videos to showcase your products, services, and premises, making your listing more attractive and engaging for potential customers.
- Encouraging customers to leave reviews on your GMB listing and responding to them in a timely and professional manner to show your commitment to customer satisfaction.

6.2 Local Keyword Research: Identifying Target Keywords for Your Geographic Area

Local keyword research is the process of identifying the most valuable and relevant keywords for your target geographic area, helping you optimise your website for local search results and attract customers from your target location. To conduct local keyword research, use keyword research tools such as Google Keyword Planner or Moz Keyword Explorer, and focus on:

- Identifying location-specific keywords, such as your city, county, or neighbourhood, along with relevant industry terms and phrases.
- Analysing the search volumes, competition, and search intent for your target local keywords to ensure

they align with your business goals and target audience.
- Creating a list of local long-tail keywords, which are longer, more specific phrases that represent a smaller but more targeted portion of search traffic.

6.3 On-Page Local SEO: Optimising Your Website for Local Search Results

Once you have identified your target local keywords, it's essential to incorporate them into your website's content, structure, and design to improve your visibility and performance in local search results. To optimise your website for local SEO, focus on:

- Including your target local keywords in your title tags, meta descriptions, header tags, URL structure, and on-page content.
- Creating high-quality, location-specific content, such as blog posts, case studies, and testimonials, that showcase your expertise and authority in your local area.
- Adding local schema markup to your website's HTML to provide search engines with more information about your business, such as its location, opening hours, and services.
- Ensuring your website is mobile-friendly and responsive, as local searchers often use their

smartphones to find and engage with nearby businesses.

In the next chapter, we'll explore the world of technical SEO, discussing the best practices and techniques for optimising your website's performance, accessibility, and indexability to ensure it ranks well in search results and provides a positive user experience.

Chapter 7: Technical SEO: Ensuring Your Website Performs Well for Users and Search Engines

In this chapter, we'll discuss technical SEO, focusing on the best practices and techniques for optimising your website's performance, accessibility, and indexability to ensure it ranks well in search results and provides a positive user experience. We'll cover topics such as site speed, mobile-friendliness, and structured data, ensuring you have the knowledge and tools to create a technically sound website that meets the expectations of both users and search engines.

7.1 Site Speed: The Importance of a Fast-Loading Website

Site speed is a critical aspect of technical SEO, as it directly impacts your website's user experience and search engine rankings. A fast-loading website can help reduce bounce rates, increase user engagement, and improve your visibility in search results. To optimise your website's site speed, focus on:

- Compressing images using tools like TinyPNG or ImageOptim to reduce their file size without compromising their quality.
- Minifying CSS and JavaScript files to eliminate unnecessary code and reduce their file size.

- Implementing browser caching and content delivery networks (CDNs) to improve page load times for repeat visitors and users in different geographic locations.
- Optimising your server response time by choosing a reliable web host and monitoring your server performance to address any issues that may arise.

7.2 Mobile-Friendliness: Catering to the Growing Mobile Audience

As more and more users access the internet from their smartphones and tablets, it's crucial to ensure your website is mobile-friendly and responsive, adapting to different devices and screen sizes to provide a seamless user experience. A mobile-friendly website can improve your search engine rankings, user engagement, and conversion rates. To optimise your website for mobile-friendliness, focus on:

- Implementing a responsive design that automatically adjusts your website's layout and content to fit different screen sizes and devices.
- Using mobile-friendly navigation and menus that are easy to use and understand on smaller screens.
- Optimising your images, videos, and other media for mobile devices to ensure they load quickly and display correctly.
- Avoiding intrusive pop-ups, overlays, and interstitials that can disrupt the user experience and lead to penalties from search engines.

7.3 Structured Data: Helping Search Engines Understand Your Content

Structured data is a form of metadata that helps search engines better understand the content of your web pages, allowing them to provide richer, more informative search results for users. Implementing structured data on your website can improve your visibility and click-through rates in search results, as well as enhance the overall user experience.

Some common types of structured data include:

- Organization: Provides information about your business, such as your name, logo, and contact details.
- Breadcrumbs: Displays a breadcrumb trail in search results, helping users understand the structure and hierarchy of your website.
- Article: Highlights the main content of your web pages, including the headline, author, and publication date.
- Product: Provides detailed information about your products, including their name, price, and availability.

To implement structured data on your website, use Google's Structured Data Markup Helper or a structured data generator tool to create the appropriate code for your content, and add it to your website's HTML.

In the next chapter, we'll dive into the world of content marketing, discussing the strategies and techniques for creating, promoting, and distributing valuable, relevant content to attract and engage your target audience and support your overall SEO goals.

Chapter 8: Content Marketing: Attracting and Engaging Your Target Audience with Valuable Content

In this chapter, we'll discuss content marketing, focusing on the strategies and techniques for creating, promoting, and distributing valuable, relevant content to attract and engage your target audience and support your overall SEO goals. We'll cover topics such as content planning, content creation, and content promotion, ensuring you have the knowledge and tools to create a successful content marketing strategy for your website.

8.1 Content Planning: Developing a Strategic Approach to Your Content

Content planning involves developing a strategic approach to your content creation, promotion, and distribution efforts, helping you ensure your content aligns with your business goals and target audience needs. To create an effective content plan, focus on:

- Identifying your target audience and their needs, interests, and pain points to ensure your content is relevant and engaging.
- Defining your content marketing goals, such as increasing brand awareness, generating leads, or improving search engine rankings.

- Conducting keyword research to identify the most valuable and relevant keywords for your target audience and industry.
- Creating a content calendar to plan and schedule your content production, promotion, and distribution efforts, ensuring you maintain a consistent and organised approach.

8.2 Content Creation: Crafting High-Quality, Valuable Content

Content creation involves crafting high-quality, valuable content that resonates with your target audience and supports your content marketing goals. To create engaging and effective content, focus on:

- Producing a variety of content formats, such as blog posts, articles, videos, infographics, and podcasts, to appeal to different audience preferences and consumption habits.
- Ensuring your content is well-researched, accurate, and informative, providing real value to your audience and establishing your expertise and authority in your industry.
- Incorporating your target keywords and SEO best practices into your content to improve its visibility and performance in search results.
- Using a clear, engaging, and relatable writing style that appeals to your target audience and encourages them to share and engage with your content.

8.3 Content Promotion: Maximising the Reach and Visibility of Your Content

Content promotion involves maximising the reach and visibility of your content, ensuring it gets in front of your target audience and generates the desired results. To effectively promote your content, focus on:

- Sharing your content on relevant social media platforms, such as Facebook, Twitter, LinkedIn, and Pinterest, to increase its reach and visibility.
- Building relationships with industry influencers, bloggers, and other relevant websites to encourage natural link building and content promotion.
- Conducting outreach campaigns to promote your content and request links, shares, or guest posting opportunities from relevant websites.
- Using paid advertising channels, such as Google Ads, Facebook Ads, or sponsored content, to reach a larger and more targeted audience.

In the next chapter, we'll explore the world of analytics and performance tracking, discussing the tools and techniques for monitoring, analysing, and optimising your SEO efforts to ensure they deliver the desired results and support your business goals.

Chapter 9: Analytics and Performance Tracking: Measuring and Optimising Your SEO Efforts

In this chapter, we'll discuss analytics and performance tracking, focusing on the tools and techniques for monitoring, analysing, and optimising your SEO efforts to ensure they deliver the desired results and support your business goals. We'll cover topics such as Google Analytics, Google Search Console, and key performance indicators (KPIs), ensuring you have the knowledge and tools to effectively track and optimise your SEO strategy.

9.1 Google Analytics: Monitoring Your Website's Traffic and User Behaviour

Google Analytics is a free, powerful tool that allows you to monitor your website's traffic, user behaviour, and performance, helping you gain valuable insights into your audience and the effectiveness of your SEO efforts. To get the most out of Google Analytics, focus on:

- Setting up and configuring Google Analytics on your website, ensuring you have access to accurate and comprehensive data.
- Exploring key metrics, such as sessions, pageviews, bounce rate, and average session duration, to better

understand your website's traffic and user engagement.
- Analysing traffic sources and channels, such as organic search, paid search, social media, and referral traffic, to identify the most effective methods for driving traffic to your website.
- Setting up goals and conversions to track the success of your SEO efforts and the impact they have on your business objectives.

9.2 Google Search Console: Gaining Insights into Your Website's Search Performance

Google Search Console is another free tool that provides valuable insights into your website's search performance, indexability, and visibility in Google search results. To effectively use Google Search Console, focus on:

- Verifying and connecting your website to Google Search Console, ensuring you have access to accurate and up-to-date data.
- Monitoring your website's index status, crawl errors, and sitemaps to ensure your content is being properly indexed and displayed in search results.
- Analysing your website's search performance, such as impressions, clicks, click-through rate (CTR), and average position, to better understand its visibility and competitiveness in search results.
- Identifying and addressing any issues or errors reported by Google Search Console, such as mobile

usability issues or structured data errors, to ensure your website is optimised for search engines and users.

9.3 Key Performance Indicators (KPIs): Tracking the Success of Your SEO Efforts

Key performance indicators (KPIs) are quantifiable metrics that help you track the success of your SEO efforts and the impact they have on your business objectives. To effectively monitor and optimise your SEO strategy, focus on:

- Defining relevant KPIs that align with your business goals and SEO objectives, such as organic traffic growth, keyword rankings, conversion rate, or return on investment (ROI).
- Regularly monitoring and analysing your KPIs to identify trends, patterns, and areas of improvement in your SEO strategy.
- Adjusting and optimising your SEO efforts based on your KPIs, ensuring you continuously improve your performance and achieve your desired results.
- Communicating your KPIs and their progress to your team and stakeholders, ensuring they understand the value and impact of your SEO efforts on your business.

In the next chapter, we'll discuss the importance of ongoing SEO maintenance and the strategies and techniques for keeping your website optimised, up-to-date, and competitive in the ever-changing world of search engine algorithms and user behaviour.

Chapter 10: Ongoing SEO Maintenance: Keeping Your Website Optimised and Competitive

In this chapter, we'll discuss the importance of ongoing SEO maintenance and the strategies and techniques for keeping your website optimised, up-to-date, and competitive in the ever-changing world of search engine algorithms and user behaviour. We'll cover topics such as algorithm updates, link building, and content updates, ensuring you have the knowledge and tools to maintain and improve your SEO efforts over time.

10.1 Staying Updated with Algorithm Changes: Adapting to the Evolving Search Landscape

Search engine algorithms are constantly evolving, with Google and other search engines frequently updating their ranking factors and criteria to provide the best possible search experience for users. To keep your website optimised and competitive, it's essential to stay updated with the latest algorithm changes and adapt your SEO strategy accordingly. Focus on:

- Following industry news and publications, such as Search Engine Land, Moz, or Search Engine Journal, to

stay informed about the latest algorithm updates and their implications.
- Regularly reviewing and updating your on-page and technical SEO practices to ensure they align with the current best practices and search engine guidelines.
- Monitoring your website's performance and rankings in search results to identify any potential issues or changes resulting from algorithm updates.

10.2 Ongoing Link Building: Continuously Building and Maintaining Your Website's Backlink Profile

Link building is an ongoing process that involves continuously building and maintaining your website's backlink profile to improve its authority, trustworthiness, and visibility in search results. To effectively manage your ongoing link building efforts, focus on:

- Creating high-quality, valuable content that naturally attracts backlinks from other websites and users.
- Engaging in outreach and relationship building with industry influencers, bloggers, and other relevant websites to promote your content and request backlinks.
- Regularly monitoring and analysing your backlink profile using tools like Ahrefs or Moz to identify new link opportunities and remove any toxic or low-quality links that may harm your website's reputation and rankings.

10.3 Updating and Refreshing Your Content: Keeping Your Website Relevant and Engaging

Content updates and refreshes are essential for maintaining your website's relevance, engagement, and performance in search results. Regularly updating your content can help ensure it remains accurate, up-to-date, and valuable to your target audience, as well as improve its visibility and rankings in search results. To effectively manage your content updates and refreshes, focus on:

- Regularly reviewing and updating your existing content to ensure it remains accurate, relevant, and up-to-date with the latest industry trends, news, and developments.
- Refreshing your content with new information, examples, case studies, or multimedia elements to keep it engaging and valuable for your audience.
- Monitoring your content's performance and engagement metrics, such as pageviews, bounce rate, and social shares, to identify any areas of improvement or opportunities for updates and refreshes.

In the next chapter, we'll discuss advanced SEO techniques and strategies that can help take your website's performance and rankings to the next level, ensuring you stay ahead of your competition and achieve your desired results.

Chapter 11: Advanced SEO Techniques: Taking Your Website's Performance to the Next Level

In this chapter, we'll discuss advanced SEO techniques and strategies that can help take your website's performance and rankings to the next level, ensuring you stay ahead of your competition and achieve your desired results. We'll cover topics such as schema markup, local SEO, and mobile-first indexing, providing you with the knowledge and tools to implement these advanced techniques and further optimise your website.

11.1 Schema Markup: Enhancing Your Search Results with Structured Data

Schema markup is a form of structured data that can be added to your website's HTML to provide search engines with additional context and information about your content, helping them display rich snippets and other enhanced search results. To effectively implement schema markup on your website, focus on:

- Identifying the most relevant schema types for your content, such as articles, products, events, or reviews, based on the Schema.org vocabulary.

- Adding the appropriate schema markup to your website's HTML using JSON-LD or Microdata formats, ensuring you follow the correct syntax and guidelines.
- Testing and validating your schema markup using Google's Structured Data Testing Tool or Rich Results Test to ensure it's correctly implemented and recognised by search engines

11.2 Local SEO: Optimising Your Website for Local Search and Visibility

Local SEO involves optimising your website and online presence for local search and visibility, ensuring your business is easily found by users searching for products or services in your area. To effectively implement local SEO strategies, focus on:

- Claiming and optimising your Google My Business listing, ensuring you provide accurate, up-to-date information about your business, such as your address, phone number, opening hours, and website.
- Incorporating local keywords and phrases into your website's content and metadata, such as your city, region, or neighbourhood, to improve its relevance and visibility in local search results.
- Earning and managing customer reviews on Google, Yelp, and other relevant platforms, as positive reviews can help improve your business's reputation, trustworthiness, and visibility in local search results.

11.3 Mobile-First Indexing: Ensuring Your Website is Optimised for Mobile Devices

Mobile-first indexing is Google's practice of prioritising the mobile version of your website when determining its rankings and visibility in search results, as more and more users are accessing the web from mobile devices. To ensure your website is optimised for mobile-first indexing, focus on:

- Implementing a responsive web design that automatically adapts to different screen sizes and devices, ensuring your website is easily accessible and usable on mobile devices.
- Optimising your website's load time and performance on mobile devices, using tools like Google's PageSpeed Insights or Lighthouse to identify and address any issues or bottlenecks.
- Ensuring your website's content, metadata, and structured data are consistent and accessible across both desktop and mobile versions, as this can impact your rankings and visibility in search results.

In the next chapter, we'll explore the role of social media in SEO and discuss strategies and techniques for leveraging social media platforms to support your SEO efforts, drive traffic to your website, and engage your target audience.

Chapter 12: Social Media and SEO: Leveraging Social Platforms to Support Your SEO Efforts

In this chapter, we'll explore the role of social media in SEO and discuss strategies and techniques for leveraging social media platforms to support your SEO efforts, drive traffic to your website, and engage your target audience. We'll cover topics such as social signals, content promotion, and social listening, providing you with the knowledge and tools to effectively integrate social media into your overall SEO strategy.

12.1 Social Signals: Understanding the Impact of Social Media on SEO

Social signals refer to the various interactions and engagements your content receives on social media platforms, such as likes, shares, comments, and retweets. While social signals may not directly impact your search rankings, they can indirectly influence your SEO efforts by:

- Increasing your content's visibility and reach, as more people share and engage with it on social media.
- Driving additional traffic to your website, as users click through to your content from social media platforms.

- Building your brand's reputation and authority, as users are more likely to trust and engage with content that has been shared and endorsed by others.

12.2 Content Promotion: Using Social Media to Drive Traffic and Engagement

Social media platforms provide an excellent opportunity to promote your content and drive traffic to your website, as well as engage with your target audience and encourage them to share and interact with your content. To effectively use social media for content promotion, focus on:

- Sharing and promoting your content on relevant social media platforms, such as Facebook, Twitter, LinkedIn, or Pinterest, ensuring you tailor your messaging and format to each platform's unique audience and requirements.
- Encouraging your audience to share and engage with your content by including social sharing buttons on your website, as well as asking for shares, comments, or feedback in your social media posts.
- Building relationships and partnerships with industry influencers, bloggers, and other relevant accounts, as they can help amplify your content's reach and credibility on social media platforms.

12.3 Social Listening: Monitoring Social Media for SEO Insights and Opportunities

Social listening involves monitoring social media platforms for conversations, trends, and feedback related to your industry, brand, or content, helping you gain valuable insights and opportunities to improve your SEO efforts. To effectively implement social listening, focus on:

- Using social listening tools, such as Hootsuite, Mention, or Brand24, to monitor relevant keywords, hashtags, and accounts on social media platforms.
- Analysing the data and insights gathered from social listening to identify trends, opportunities, or areas of improvement in your SEO strategy, such as popular topics, keywords, or content formats.
- Engaging with your audience on social media, responding to their comments, questions, or feedback, as well as participating in industry-related discussions and groups to build your brand's reputation, authority, and visibility.

In the next chapter, we'll discuss the importance of continuous learning and professional development in SEO, as well as provide resources and recommendations for staying up-to-date with the latest trends, best practices, and developments in the industry.

Chapter 13: Continuous Learning and Professional Development in SEO

In this chapter, we'll discuss the importance of continuous learning and professional development in SEO, as well as provide resources and recommendations for staying up-to-date with the latest trends, best practices, and developments in the industry. By investing in your SEO education and skills, you'll be better equipped to adapt to the ever-changing search landscape, optimise your website, and achieve your desired results.

13.1 The Importance of Continuous Learning in SEO

As search engines and user behaviour continue to evolve, it's essential for SEO professionals and website owners to stay informed about the latest trends, best practices, and algorithm updates in the industry. Continuous learning not only helps you stay competitive and maintain your website's performance and rankings but also enables you to:

- Identify new opportunities and strategies for optimising your website and driving traffic.
- Adapt to changes in search engine algorithms and guidelines, minimising the risk of penalties or ranking drops.
- Develop a comprehensive understanding of SEO, allowing you to make more informed decisions and implement more effective strategies.

13.2 Recommended SEO Resources and Publications

There are numerous resources and publications available to help you stay informed about the latest SEO trends, best practices, and developments, including:

- Industry blogs and websites, such as Search Engine Land, Moz, Search Engine Journal, Ahrefs, and SEMrush, which regularly publish articles, guides, and news updates on various SEO topics.
- SEO conferences and events, such as BrightonSEO, SMX, and Pubcon, which offer opportunities to learn from industry experts, network with fellow professionals, and discover new tools and techniques.
- Online courses and certifications, such as those offered by Google, Moz, or SEMrush, which can help you develop your SEO skills and knowledge, as well as demonstrate your expertise to clients or employers.

13.3 Networking and Community Involvement in the SEO Industry

In addition to staying informed about the latest SEO trends and best practices, it's also essential to build relationships and engage with other professionals in the industry. Networking and community involvement can help you:

- Gain valuable insights and advice from fellow SEO professionals, as well as share your own experiences and knowledge.
- Stay informed about the latest industry news, trends, and updates, as well as discover new tools, techniques, and opportunities.
- Build your professional network and reputation, which can lead to potential partnerships, collaborations, or job opportunities.

To effectively network and engage with the SEO community, consider participating in industry forums, such as SEO Chat or WebmasterWorld, joining SEO-focused groups on social media platforms like LinkedIn or Facebook, and attending local SEO meetups or events in your area.

In the next chapter, we'll recap the key takeaways from this SEO guide, providing you with a comprehensive overview of the strategies, techniques, and best practices discussed throughout the book, as well as actionable steps for implementing and improving your SEO efforts.

Chapter 14: SEO Guide Recap: Key Takeaways and Actionable Steps

In this final chapter, we'll recap the key takeaways from this SEO guide, providing you with a comprehensive overview of the strategies, techniques, and best practices discussed throughout the book, as well as actionable steps for implementing and improving your SEO efforts. By following these recommendations and continuously investing in your SEO education and skills, you'll be better positioned to achieve your desired results and maintain your website's performance and rankings in the ever-changing search landscape.

Key Takeaways and Actionable Steps:
1. **SEO Fundamentals:**
    - Understand the importance of SEO and how it can impact your website's visibility, traffic, and conversions.
    - Familiarise yourself with essential SEO concepts, terms, and best practices.
    - Conduct thorough keyword research to identify relevant, high-traffic, and low-competition keywords for your website.

2. **On-Page SEO:**
    - Optimise your website's content, metadata, and structure to improve its relevance, accessibility, and user experience.

- Implement internal and external linking strategies to enhance your website's authority, navigation, and visibility in search results.
- Monitor and improve your website's load time and performance using tools like Google's PageSpeed Insights or Lighthouse.

3. **Off-Page SEO:**
   - Develop a comprehensive backlink strategy, focusing on earning high-quality, relevant, and authoritative backlinks from trusted sources.
   - Utilise content marketing, guest blogging, and influencer outreach to build relationships, earn backlinks, and increase your website's visibility and reach.
   - Monitor your backlink profile and disavow any harmful or spammy links that may negatively impact your website's rankings and reputation.

4. **Technical SEO:**
   - Ensure your website is accessible and crawlable by search engines, implementing XML sitemaps, robots.txt files, and proper URL structures.
   - Monitor and fix any crawl errors, broken links, or duplicate content issues that may negatively impact your website's performance and rankings.
   - Implement structured data and schema markup to enhance your website's search results and provide additional context and information to search engines.

5. **Advanced SEO Techniques:**

- Incorporate schema markup, local SEO, and mobile-first indexing strategies to further optimise your website and improve its performance in search results.
- Leverage social media platforms to support your SEO efforts, drive traffic, and engage your target audience.
- Participate in continuous learning and professional development to stay informed about the latest SEO trends, best practices, and developments.

By following the recommendations and strategies discussed in this guide, you'll be well on your way to improving your website's SEO performance, driving more traffic, and achieving your desired results. Remember, SEO is an ongoing process that requires patience, persistence, and continuous improvement. Stay committed to your efforts, and you'll be rewarded with long-term success in the competitive world of search engine optimisation.

Chapter 15: Measuring SEO Success and Adjusting Your Strategy

In this chapter, we'll discuss the importance of measuring your SEO success and adjusting your strategy based on data-driven insights. We'll cover various key performance indicators (KPIs) to track, tools for measuring your website's performance, and strategies for adjusting your SEO efforts to achieve your desired results.

15.1 Key Performance Indicators (KPIs) to Track

Tracking the right KPIs is crucial for measuring your SEO success and understanding the impact of your efforts on your website's performance. Some important KPIs to track include:

- Organic traffic: The number of users who visit your website through organic search results, which is a primary indicator of your SEO success.
- Keyword rankings: The position of your targeted keywords in search engine results pages (SERPs), which can help you understand the effectiveness of your keyword strategy and on-page optimisation.
- Bounce rate: The percentage of users who leave your website after visiting only one page, which can indicate issues with your website's user experience, content quality, or relevance.
- Conversion rate: The percentage of users who complete a desired action on your website, such as

making a purchase, signing up for a newsletter, or submitting a contact form, which helps you understand the effectiveness of your SEO efforts in driving conversions.

15.2 Tools for Measuring Your Website's Performance

Several tools can help you measure your website's SEO performance and track your KPIs, including:

- Google Analytics: A comprehensive analytics tool that provides insights into your website's traffic, user behaviour, and conversion rates, allowing you to track your organic traffic, bounce rate, and other KPIs.
- Google Search Console: A free tool that offers valuable data on your website's search performance, including keyword rankings, click-through rates, and crawl errors.
- Ahrefs, Moz, or SEMrush: SEO platforms that provide a wide range of tools for tracking your website's backlinks, keyword rankings, and other SEO-related metrics, as well as insights and recommendations for improving your strategy.

15.3 Adjusting Your SEO Strategy Based on Data-Driven Insights

Measuring your SEO success and tracking your KPIs allows you to make data-driven decisions and adjustments to your strategy, ensuring you continually improve your website's performance and achieve your desired results. Some strategies for adjusting your SEO efforts based on data-driven insights include:

- Refining your keyword strategy: Analyse your keyword rankings and search traffic to identify high-performing keywords, as well as opportunities for targeting new or underperforming keywords.
- Optimising your content: Assess your website's bounce rate, time on page, and conversion rates to identify issues or areas of improvement in your content, such as quality, relevance, or user experience.
- Enhancing your backlink profile: Monitor your website's backlinks and domain authority to identify opportunities for earning new, high-quality backlinks or disavowing harmful or spammy links.

By continually measuring your SEO success and adjusting your strategy based on data-driven insights, you'll be better positioned to optimise your website, stay ahead of your competition, and achieve your desired results in the ever-changing search landscape.

Dear Reader,

As we reach the conclusion of "The SEO Guide 2023", I'd like to extend my heartfelt thanks and appreciation for joining me on this comprehensive journey through the world of search engine optimisation. It has been a pleasure to share my knowledge, insights, and passion for SEO with you, and I trust that the strategies and best practices within these pages will serve as invaluable tools in your quest to optimise your website and achieve your desired results.

Remember, SEO is a continuous and ever-evolving process that requires dedication, patience, and adaptability. By staying informed, investing in your education, and embracing a data-driven approach, you'll be well-prepared to navigate the ever-changing landscape of search engines and maintain a competitive edge.

I wish you the very best of luck in your SEO endeavours and eagerly anticipate hearing about your successes. Your commitment to mastering this crucial aspect of online success is commendable, and I have no doubt that you are well on your way to realising your goals.

Once again, thank you for choosing "The SEO Guide 2023", and here's to your online success!

Warm regards,

Adam J Broadhead

Author of "The SEO Guide 2023"

Printed in Great Britain
by Amazon